DEDICATED TO MY FATHER
ROMUALD MICHNIEWICZ

AN OFFICER AND A SOLDIER

Footsteps in the snow: A true story of one family's journey out of Siberia

Front Cover: Rom Michniewicz, 1939
Layout and design: Paul Martinez

Published by:
Romaste Inc
2218 Wilshire Blvd., #1070
Santa Monica, CA 90403

ISBN-13: 978-0-615-33846-0
ISBN-10:   0-615-33846-1

First Edition
Second Printing

Visit us online at www.roma-king.com

Footsteps In the Snow

by Roma King

Chapter 1

ESCAPE

It was almost midnight, the time they had set for their escape. They were being held as prisoners of war in Riga, Latvia, in an old castle that was surrounded by a moat on three sides. A wide river flowed behind the castle.

Germans had crossed the border into Poland just four months before without declaring war, and the unprepared country was defeated in just one month. The officers and soldiers were taken prisoner and transported to this remote castle in Riga, which now served as a prison for the prisoners of war.

Conditions here were hard, one skimpy meal a day called soup but only resembling such. Cold cement floors, no shoes, no heat, and this was in the middle of a hard Northern European winter.

Five young officers, prisoners, were huddled in the corner in deep discussion about how to get back home to help defend their country. They had no news from the underground army in Poland but knew that they must still be fighting the enemy who had overrun Poland in September 1939.

Tonight was the night they decided to break out of their confinement.

It was New Year's Eve. Soon the guards would be celebrating. There would be drinking among them for sure, so this would be an ideal opportunity that might not come again. This was the night destined for escape.

The officers chosen to undertake this venture were young, very fit, and ready for any sacrifice to help their country in need. Rom was the athlete among them, and the others all placed their hopes in him.

It was arranged that when the clock struck midnight and toasts began, the five prisoners would scale the steep wall down to the river. There were no guards on that side. The men would swim across the river and then run about a mile into the forest and on through the woods to cross the border into Poland.

For a few months now the snow had covered the ground, and the river waters were freezing cold. The prisoners were aware that after swimming across they must quickly strip down to their shorts to avoid the clothes being quick-frozen to their bodies. The plan was then to run as fast as they could into the shelter of the forest to have a chance of escaping in case of pursuit. The crossing completed, they must all go their separate ways and hopefully avoid capture when crossing the border into Poland.

According to plan, they all managed to get as far as the river, and then it was each man on his own. Rom, although a strong swimmer, struggled against the freezing water currents, but he made it. The fate of the others remains unknown.

As soon as he came out of the water and stripped, Rom ran with his wet bundle of clothing toward the forest. He ran backward so that his footsteps in the snow would make it appear that someone had gone in the opposite direction and confuse the guards in case of pursuit.

Among the trees, he stopped to put on his wet shirt and then continued running toward the Polish border, avoiding probable border patrols and hiding on sighting them.

Many hours later and almost at the border he stopped to wipe his brow, when suddenly he felt a grip of iron on his thigh. A German shepherd was holding him. Rom thought, "I can snap his neck," but behind him he heard a Russian voice call out, "Stop, or

I will shoot!" A Russian soldier huffing and exhausted, his green uniform dark with sweat from the pursuit, came up with his rifle pointed at Rom. Rom raised his hands. The thoughts passing through his mind were: "I can talk to this soldier, he looks so young; he couldn't be more than twenty. I shall tell him I am trying to get back to my wife and home for New Year's, just fifty kilometers on the other side of the Soviet-Polish border."

Rom was making progress and even could tell that the young man believed him. Of course, it helped to speak the German language, so things began to look up.

Just then, the change of patrol was approaching with a lieutenant in front of a small marching column. Things changed rapidly. The lieutenant did not believe any such story and kept saying, "You are a spy," and nothing could change his mind. Rom was escorted between six armed guards to the border and given over to the enemy authorities as a spy, accused of "crossing the border at night during war conditions and without any documents."

Who else but a spy would attempt that?

Rom was handcuffed and put onto the army convoy truck going to Moscow. According to the border patrol he was a "political spy" and so he was being transported to prison.

The journey to Moscow took a couple of days. On arrival the prisoner was handed over to the guards of the Moscow Political Prison.

Rom was interrogated daily, but the guards learned nothing as there was nothing to tell, except that he had escaped from prison in Latvia and was crossing the border to reach his wife and home during the festive holiday season. But Rom could not make them believe that. After being questioned without any results, he was thrown into a solitary-confinement cell for thirty days, the dreaded experience of every prisoner who receives such a sentence.

The cell was five by six feet and bare except for wooden planks on the wet cement floor. The walls were dripping icy water from the freezing conditions outside. The door to the cell had some cracks in it, and through these Rom glimpsed the only daylight that came into the cell.

Here only the constant exercise saved Rom's life. He could not even stretch out on the wooden planks, as he was five feet eleven inches tall, but he knew that unless he kept moving, jumping, running in place, he would certainly freeze.

Most of the night was spent in exercising, and only when he heard the guards coming with breakfast, tea and a thick slice of bread, in the morning did he sit cross-legged on the planks. After a few days he heard the guards betting how many more days he could survive such conditions. But each morning, to their amazement, they found him sitting cross-legged on the wooden planks.

The nourishment was scant, and the cold was penetrating. Rom held out maybe twenty some days—he lost count—but he noticed he was becoming very swollen. Even around his eyes the skin puffed up so that he could not see well through the slits. Exercising became painful, and he finally stopped it altogether, as his body ballooned to extraordinary proportions and he lost the energy to move.

At last one morning the guards announced, "You made it!" and pulled him out of the cell. He walked with the greatest difficulty, due to the swelling of his body. His eyes were almost shut.

He was taken directly to the infirmary. Curtains were drawn around his bed. It seemed no one cared and that death was inevitable.

The next morning a young doctor was making the rounds of the wards and asked the nurse, "Who is behind those curtains?" The reply was, "Just a Polish officer, but he is dying, has maybe another day."

The curtains parted, and a voice in his native tongue, Polish, asked Rom if he could hear him. When Rom nodded, the voice then told him to take heart because something that would help his condition would be prescribed. The doctor returned with a tumbler full of cod liver oil, and with the help of the nurse Rom slowly drank it. Each day the same procedure took place: a tumbler full of cod liver oil was Rom's daily food ration. In a couple of weeks the swelling slowly receded, and Rom, though very weak, was able to start getting out of bed and slowly walking again. The doctor told him he would request Rom's transfer to be an assistant in the infirmary; otherwise, if he were sent back to his prison cell, he would surely die.

The doctor told the prison authorities that Rom had some medical training and could be useful in the infirmary. Thus, Rom remained at the hospital, slowly getting back his strength and assisting in the hospital wards.

Chapter 2

THE DAY THE RUSSIANS TOOK ANTONI, AGNIESZKA, JANINA, AND BABY ROMA TO SIBERIA

A flashback.

When World War II began, the Germans were bombing all larger cities throughout Poland. Rom advised his wife Janina to take the baby and nanny and move from Wilno to his father's estate in Stare Swieciany about seventy kilometers away. The town house was closed down.

Janina, Roma, and her nanny traveled by train to the estate and settled with the Michniewicz family. Antoni, Rom's father, raised horses, and life on the estate was good and plentiful.

With the advent of war, it was easier on those living in the country than it was for those in the city. At least there was no shortage of food yet, and on the whole it was still peaceful, so that life went on pretty much as usual.

The peasants went about their daily work that needed to be done in the stables and the fields. The winter was approaching, the harvest was in progress, and all seemed quite peaceful and still.

Until the month of February 1940.

Everything changed then for the Michniewicz family, as well as for hundreds of thousands of other Polish families throughout the eastern part of Poland.

The Russian army crossed the border of Poland under the guise of "friendship and help" for Poles against the German army advancing through that country. Meanwhile, the Soviet Union made a pact with Germany to annihilate Poland from the map of Europe and divide the spoils. There would no longer be a Poland on the map. The new allies would see to it.

Unexpected allies, both bent on the destruction of Poland.

As soon as her troops crossed the border into Poland, the Soviet Union began to occupy the territories and transport the people from the cities and the countryside alike. Anyone they considered a threat to them or who was educated or affluent was sent to the depth of Siberian wilderness.

Political and social personalities were detained and taken to Siberia. Members of parliament and senators, local mayors and heads of district administrations, eminent landowners and owners of factories, all people engaged in official activities, chief justices, priests, public prosecutors, simple policemen—all were arrested.

Thus the number of people arrested or disappearing from their homes steadily increased. All these people were indicted for their normal loyal service to the Polish state under those paragraphs of the Soviet Code that referred to counterrevolution. The fact of serving one's country was, because it was capitalist, interpreted by Soviet justice as a crime against the interests of revolution and the international proletariat.

Later, after the war, when the statistics were assembled, it was ascertained that the Poles from the eastern provinces who were deported to the Soviet Union, counting prisoners of war and civilians, amounted to between 1.5 and 1.6 million people.

Members of the Michniewicz family were among those deported in February 1940. The estate of Antoni Michniewicz lay only fifty kilometers from the border. Hence it was one of the first to be occupied, with the family transported to Siberia.

On February 10 at about 2:00 A.M. suddenly the household was awakened by the intense barking of the German shepherds who were let loose nightly to protect the grounds.

Antoni, who had only just finished some estate paperwork and was getting ready to go to bed, quickly went out to see what was making the dogs so angry. Before he could call them to him, a few shots rang out and the dogs lay dead. They were his pride and joy, a part of his large family consisting of people and animals that had bonded strongly over the years spent together.

Antoni quickly ran into the house to get his gun, but already a platoon of soldiers on horseback was approaching the manor. The lieutenant leading them got off his horse with a pistol in hand. Unceremoniously he marched into the manor house demanding to see the head of the family.

After Antoni came forward, he was asked where his son and the rest of his family were. Janina awoke from deep sleep, and before she could get out of bed she was facing the Russian officer and the enemy.

"How dare you, sir, enter my bedroom!" she protested, putting as much arrogance in her voice as she could muster.

The lieutenant answered her quickly: "I have orders to take you to the station. Please hurry and dress. You may each take one suitcase only with essentials," he instructed.

Janina answered with false bravado, "I am not going anywhere!"

"Well," the officer replied, "my orders are simple. Either you come with us or I am to shoot you here if you refuse."

Antoni entered at that moment and told the officer that he would assist his daughter-in-law. He explained to Janina that there was no recourse; they must go with the soldiers.

The servants proved their loyalty to the family in this hour of need. The maid tried to help dress Janina, who was so distraught she was trying to put a dress on over her nightgown. The maid also put all the jewelry she could on Janina's hands and then pulled gloves over them. She cautioned Janina to leave the gloves on while on the train so that the people would not see the rings and rob her of them. Maybe where they were going, these rings would be a good exchange for food, she advised Janina.

In the kitchen, while a basket of provisions was being assembled, members of the family were told by the lieutenant in charge that they must hurry not to miss the train.

Meanwhile the nanny quickly dressed little Roma in furs and shawls—after all, it was February and the height of winter. Janina came out dressed in her long fur and muffled against the cold too. The officer absolutely refused to take the nanny, although she begged to go with the child. He took the child away from her, pushing her roughly aside. Janina, seeing her little girl in the arms of the officer, ran quickly to take Roma away from him, shouting, "Do not touch my child! You are the enemy!"

He answered gently: "Lady, I am not your enemy. I am just following my orders."

In less than an hour Antoni (Rom's father), seventy-two years old; Agnieszka (Rom's grandmother), eighty-nine; Janina (Rom's wife), twenty-two; and baby Roma (Rom's daughter), five months old, were all bundled into the sleigh and transported with speed to the train station. There they were packed into cattle cars with only narrow little windows close to the roofs. The train started. The journey to Siberia had begun.

No one who has not experienced the hopelessness of such a situation can fathom the thoughts crossing the minds of these passengers finding themselves packed closely into cattle trains among hundreds of strangers bound for Siberia. Antoni thought to himself, "I know the language well; I know all about the animals, the maladies that befall them; I can still work. I can make enough to feed us."

Agnieszka thought, "Well, it could have been worse; they could have taken just Janina and the baby and then both of them would surely perish. At least I can still cook and take care of the baby if they put Janina to work."

Janina sat in silent despair crying most of the time and thinking: "We are going to a certain death, I know it; everyone knows that if they send you to Siberia, you will never return from there. I will never see my parents or my husband, and should Antoni and Agnieszka die, I will never manage alone, so this is the end."

While other family members had their silent thoughts, five-month-old Roma just smiled, ate everything that was given to her, and entertained herself happily, not worrying at all about anything. She was always considered a very good baby.

The journey through Siberia to their final destination lasted over two weeks. Sometimes the monotony of bare landscape as far as the eye could see and at other times high Ural mountains— everything was covered thickly by snow at this time of the year. It would have been beautiful to see it all under different circumstances.

They were fed once a day only, minimum rations: a tumbler of thin soup and a thick slice of black bread per person. The provisions taken from home were exhausted after the first three days. Little Roma managed to eat hers and at least half of her mother's daily soup rations. Janina made do with whatever was left plus sharing with Antoni and Agnieszka their portions.

During the two-week journey into the depths of Siberia, every time the train stopped at some tiny station, mostly only a shack in the wilderness, the uniformed guards counted off thirty some people and told them to get off the train, as this was their destination. Then the train moved on.

With few people left on the train, the Michniewicz family had reached the furthest eastern frontier of Siberia when their group was brusquely told, "Get off!" The deserted station was very small, only a platform with a shack.

After getting off the train, everyone squeezed into the small shack, filling it up totally. The stationmaster, if one could call him that, announced to the frozen, frightened little group that they had arrived at Kolkhoz X labor camp, near Bullayevo, a small town some forty kilometers away, close to Verkhovansk.

The disembarked travelers were told that they had been transported there to work on the farms to supply Russian troops at the front with provisions. The local farmers had been called up for service in the army, and hence there was a shortage of labor, so field hands on the farms were badly needed.

They were told further that they would be billeted with different peasant families in the village, and that all would get some daily rations of food in return for their work in the fields.

Soon the peasants from the village started to arrive. Each chose two or three people out of the little group to take back to the village. A strong, middle-aged woman came up to Antoni and asked, "And why did they take you, Grandpa, and the old grandmother? You two are too old to work, but come, I   will   take you to share my home."

"I don't know why they took us," Antoni told the woman, "and they also took with us my son's wife and the baby. Could you accommodate all of us?" She hesitated but after a while said, "Why not? We will manage. Come."

The poor Russian people had good hearts, and they helped the new arrivals as much as they could.

Each of the village cottages consisted of just two rooms, and the toilet was outside. To one big room, which normally served as a bedroom, dining room, and kitchen all in one, the woman took the family of four.

By the wall was a wide wooden bench with hay for a mattress and some tattered blankets. The woman indicated that these could be for Janina and the baby. A brick shelf built over the oven, where the bread was baked, was the size of a double bed, and the woman assigned this to the two elderly people, while she would sleep in the corner opposite from Janina on another, similar wooden bench.

During the day the benches were dragged to the square table in the center of the room, and the area then became a dining room.

Imagine the difference in circumstances for these "arrivals" just in the two weeks since leaving Poland and their comfortable manor house. Janina cried and cried and seemed to be in total shock at the situation, quite unable to cope.

There was one other room in the cottage through which all entered and which had a bare clay floor. Here all the animals of the household were kept once the weather became cold. These consisted of one old cow, one goat, about a dozen chickens, and a dog—the entire wealth of this household.

The woman lived alone since her husband had been conscripted into the army a couple of years earlier, and they had no children.

The next day all deportees had to report early to the kolkhoz, or collective labor farm, where they would be assigned work in the fields. All were given shovels and told to dig up the soil for the spring planting. Janina tried as hard as she could, putting all her weight on her shovel, but barely made a dent in the snow-covered, frozen steppe soil. The overseer told her she was of no use in the fields and instead would have to take care of the children of mothers who would be working there. Antoni and Agnieszka were dismissed because of their age. They could take care of baby Roma.

And so life in Siberia settled into a routine.

The able-bodied worked in the fields from sunup to sundown. Janina took care of seven children ranging in ages from three to nine. In her beautiful soprano voice she sang songs she knew, told them endless stories she had heard or read, and taught them the games she had played as a child.

Antoni became known as a "vet." Peasants often came to ask him to look at an ailing cow or a lame horse. Having spent his en-

tire life on his estate surrounded by domestic animals and especially horses, Antoni had much knowledge and could really help
the farmers there. As payment he got a sack of potatoes from time
to time, or a piece of meat occasionally, and some vegetables in
season.

Agnieszka took care of the house and baby Roma. Great-
grandmother was a marvel in the kitchen. She could make soup
with just a potato and some weeds that grew wild, and she knew
of more potato dishes to make than anyone living, I am sure. Almost daily, Janina got some vegetables and a liter of milk as her
payment for looking after the children of the working mothers
and thus contributed to the family provisions. And so they were
surviving.

In springtime in the area behind the cottage they lived in, Antoni planted carrots, peas, onions, tomatoes, and potatoes so that
the family would have vegetables of their own to supplement their
provisions. Agnieszka made an excellent jam by cooking carrots
on a slow flame until they became a smooth, even orange paste.
It resembled quite well apricot jam and was good on a thick slice
of freshly baked brown bread. There was no butter or sugar to be
had during the family's entire stay in Siberia.

Agnieszka could bake excellent bread. She also knew all about
and gathered the eatable mushrooms and wild berries in the deep
forest close by. The mushrooms she dried by the fireplace or in
the sun to be used in winter months, and berries made great pies,
jams, and pierogi (dough squares filled with fruit, folded into tri-
angles, and then boiled in water).

Each of the precious rings Janina had brought with her from
home, thanks to the cleverness of the maid back at their manor
house, now bought the family a couple of big sacks of flour in

the nearby town of Bullayevo and sometimes even some meat.

One day, taking a large basket, Great-grandmother Agnieszka went into the forest to gather mushrooms. The sun was setting when Antoni came home from his work and noticed that she had not yet returned. He became very worried. He knew the forest was treacherous and after sunset became very dark amid tall forest trees, and so it was very easy to get lost there. The forest, so the peasants there said, had bottomless wells and quicksand patches, to which someone not aware of the dangers could easily fall victim.

Antoni went looking for Agnieszka first through the village, asking if anyone had seen Babuszka (grandmother), but no one had. The villagers quickly formed a large group of volunteers to go with Antoni into the forest to look for Agnieszka.

Meanwhile Agnieszka returned with her big basket full of mushrooms. Being told that there was a search party out to find her, she quickly hid the basket outside amid the stacks of firewood. She knew that Antoni would be very angry with her for not returning from the forest before sunset and for sure would take out his wrath on the mushrooms. Antoni had a temper when crossed, and he was liable to trample them into the ground. She must have known him well, for when he returned, satisfied that Great-grandmother was fine, he began looking everywhere for those mushrooms. But he never did look amid the firewood in the back of the cottage.

Over those years in Siberia, the monotony of life was broken only by the change of the seasons.

Siberian summers were short but very beautiful, warm and sunny, sometimes quite hot, but with the dry heat of the desert.

The steppes, covered with tall green grass hiding brilliant blue cornflowers, poppies of every color glistening in the sun, and multitudes of wildflowers, were indeed a sight to behold. Little Roma could run now and enjoyed getting into tall grasses, which hid her completely from the panic-stricken adults looking for her. The smell of the grass was unforgettable.

Autumn was the beloved season of the peasant. The work was almost completed. After the harvest took place, the produce was stored in barns and basements in readiness for the winter. The vegetables were pickled. The mushrooms, plentiful in the forests surrounding the village, were dried in the sun and saved for winter stews. The berries were picked and turned into jams and compotes, which were stored in the basement. It was a season of relative plenty and joy.

The Russian peasants, usually optimistic, believed that things would somehow get better soon. They gathered each evening after the work in the fields was done and made fine music, even though their instruments were often homemade. The sounds of singing and dancing resounded in the surrounding fields and forest every night.

* * *

Here I have to tell a side story about little Roma's first job. Roma was over two now, following other children, running here and there, playing freely in the fields among the harvesters with Great-grandmother Agnieszka, keeping her always in her sight. To her family's horror, she was beginning to speak the Russian language better than Polish, always playing with the kolkhozniks' (farm laborers') children.

One afternoon Roma stopped to watch women sorting potatoes, which had just been dug out and lay in big heaps by the roadside. Women were sorting the good ones to one side and the bad ones to the other. Good ones were without rot or cuts by the hoe from being dug out of the ground. Those were for human consumption, while the damaged ones were put in a separate stack for the animals' winter feed.

A couple of women saw the child watching them carefully, so they jokingly asked her, "Do you want to work? Start putting good ones here and bad ones there." They showed Roma how a good one looked and how "tfu! tfu!" the bad ones looked. Roma went to work and tirelessly kept at it quite a while. Many women noticed the child doing a good job and working long and patiently, so they put in her apron ten big potatoes to take home. "Tell your mother you earned them," they coached her.

Roma proudly took them to her cottage and put them by the door. She showed them to Antoni, Agnieszka, and Janina as soon as each one came home, telling them that she had "earned" them. Antoni shed a few tears, overwhelmed that the child not yet three years old was already earning food for the family.

However, Roma did not want "her" potatoes, which she had earned, eaten!

A few days passed, and it took Grandfather's explanation that the potatoes would rot and become "tfu! tfu!," and be given to the animals, for the child to allow her earnings to be eaten up. After she was persuaded, everyone praised the provisions as they consumed them, thanking her for her memorable contribution to the household.

* * *

Siberia in winter was covered with a thick mantle of snow, often six to ten feet deep. Everywhere the people looked was white, and snow kept falling more and more. The peasants built sleighs, strong and colorful, and the children were seen on the hills around pulling their sleighs up and then sliding down shrieking with joy, their faces red and shining with excitement.

The domestic animals during this coldest season were taken inside to share the space in the cottage with their masters. A typical home of the labor camp (kolkhoz) villagers consisted of one room for the people and one for the animals. Snowbound indoors, women spun wool, embroidered, sewed, and knitted, while men mended their tools.

There was always an abundance of work in every season. On Sundays the peasants gathered in the village hall, or *swietlica*. The village musicians played while others danced and sang until late, and they were happy.

Happiness is a state of mind, after all.

Spring followed. The snow melted, and the ground once more was prepared for new seeds to plant. The world seemed to be waking up after the long winter sleep, and the new cycle began.

Chapter 3

LIFE IN SIBERIA

The daily routine did not vary much in the kolkhoz. Life was very hard, and hunger was a constant companion to the exiles. People went to work in the fields before sunrise, and came back at sunset. They put in long, demanding hours each day just to earn enough food to feed their families. Their wants did not go beyond that as everyone who wanted to eat, however meager daily rations were allocated per person, had first to work. The motto was "no work - no food." If you couldn't work because of illness you had to depend on others to give you a small amount of their daily rations. Mother Russia does not feed those who cannot work.

After being in the kolkhoz almost a year, Antoni got a night job guarding sheep from wolves, which were frequently killing the village live stock. He acquired a dog to give him warning and a strong heavy pole to swing at the wolves. He would keep a fire burning all night to keep the wolves at bay and, while guarding the sheep didn't allow him to sleep much, he would rest in a three-sided shelter he made for himself inside the sheep pen. Antoni was paid with a small sack of potatoes, and four pounds of meat whenever a pig or a sheep was slaughtered in the kolkhoz. This was a big addition to the family's food locker. Occasionally a sack of flour or even some old clothing would come his way as additional payment, and he also managed to supplement the family's food from a small vegetable garden he cultivated behind their cottage.

* * *

Hunger, dysentery and lice were the three curses of Siberia, which no one escaped, resident or newcomer alike. Life seemed hopeless, many died of dysentery, typhus or lung diseases; yet most survived in this nightmare and most never left it.

Tiny white head lice covered every hair, three to six thick, of every human being, man, woman or child. Heads looked as if they were sprinkled heavily with salt, so thickly were lice settled on them. Twice a week, sometimes more, the heads were cleaned with gasoline, the only available 'help' in Siberia for such a pest. Yet the gasoline only killed half of the lice inhabitants, and stunned the other half. Then the hair was combed with fine-tooth combs, made of wood by kolkhoz-villagers, to try and clean the hair of lice. Hair was cut, often shaved all together, but then living and working in such close proximity, it became impossible to conquer lice totally. It was a never ending cycle.

Antoni was always thinking how he could maintain the family's larder: how to get some butter or lard to supplement the meager diet for the toddler Roma, so she would grow up strong. He realized that he could make use of his knowledge of treating illness in both humans and animals. He told the kolkhoz residents that he could cure their dysentery, a devastating illness that most of them suffered from, most of the time

Antoni knew some herbs growing abundantly in the forests that were good for soothing a sore stomach, and he knew that a spoonful of warm melted butter could serve to tighten the stool. He would tell the patient that, in addition to his mixture of herbs he needed a tablespoon of butter to create his remedy for them. This was the way to get a teaspoon of butter for the child, who now, at two did not even know what butter tasted like.

When patients arrived with a little piece of butter (no doubt stolen), he would tell them to wait outside on the bench while he would prepare the medicine. He would go inside and put half the butter aside for the toddler, and would melt the other half to mix with some finely chopped soothing herb. The patient would drink this warm mixture and, being an effective remedy, after a few such treatments would feel much better

Siberia required a tough and cunning nature in order to survive it.

* * *

Life in the kolkhoz was very primitive. There were no toilets when Antoni arrived there and in all weather villagers went into the surrounding woods or used a bedpan.

Antoni set about building the first outside 'out-house'. He dug a deep hole and fortified it with wooden boards on all sides. For privacy, he set strong poles a short distance apart, and threaded long tree branches between the poles to form a wall the height of a man. This structure was made complete with a door made in similar fashion, hinged with a rope to one side and latched with a loop to the other.

When the kolkhoz people saw this convenience, only 20 steps behind the cottage instead of having to track all the way to the edge of the forest, everyone wanted to have one. They no doubt remember to this day the grandfather who built their first outdoor conveniences - and Antoni found himself with yet another job which added substantially to the food account for his family; he was now even able to share food with some of the poorest families.

* * *

Acquiring water for drinking or washing was not a simple matter either. There was no such thing as running water and Janina and Antoni had to carry water in buckets from the river some distance away. A long pole was rested on the shoulders, like a yoke, and a bucket was suspended from the handle on each end. Balancing the pails and holding them steady while carrying the water home had to be mastered. Often one third of the water spilled out with the swaying of the buckets while walking. This "water routine" had to be repeated several times a day to meet the needs of drinking, cooking and bathing for the family of four. In winter, however, they could just scoop fresh snow close to home and melt it. There are always hidden blessings in every season.

Before winters set in with temperatures below -30°C, Antoni went into the forest every few days and often with Janina to gather firewood so a heating and cooking fire could be maintained through the long winter months. He would cut down some trees and chop them up. Then the wood was loaded into makeshift sleighs and both he and Janina would put on harnesses like horses and drag them home. Antoni, of course, pulled a larger sleigh and Janina a much smaller one; still, it was extremely hard work both for an old man and a young woman weighing 104 lbs.

* * *

At Christmas, although food was always in short supply, Antoni decided that they should try to make as good a Christmas as they possibly could, and invite all the Polish exiles to have a traditional Christmas meal. Little Roma would enjoy it now, as she was aware and learning quickly about her world.

Preparations began weeks before. Somehow Antoni and Agnieszka managed to acquire things for each of the 12 traditional courses for the Wigilia (Christmas Eve) meal. More than 30 adult exiles and eleven children of various age were accommodated in the small cottage where the Michniewicz family lived.

Antoni went to the forest and cut down a Christmas tree which was then decorated with little rag dolls that Agnieszka and Janina made to be given as presents for the girls, and Antoni made whistles and flutes for the boys, so each child would have a present hanging on the tree.

After the supper, Christmas carols were sung by all, led by the beautiful soprano voice of Janina.

It was a night to remember with joy for the rest of the year.

* * *

Without Agnieszka's and Antoni's help Janina could never have managed to survive with a small child. In addition to 'taking care of children in the fields' while their mothers worked, Janina embroidered scarves for the ladies of the village in the evenings and on Sundays. They brought her material and colored threads and each one wanted a scarf with embroidered flowers, birds, and leaves just like her neighbor had. The scarves became very popular, and a jug of milk and small sack of potatoes came as payment for each one. Other villagers asked Janina to sew pants or skirts, which she did by taking apart 'old' tattered clothing to use as a pattern for cutting the pieces out of new material and often hand sewing smaller garments.

Once Janina was even asked by a policeman's wife to make her a large bedspread, like an eiderdown, with thick wads of cotton spread between the top and bottom layers. Janina had never made an eiderdown before but thought "How difficult can that be?" Of course she took the job, did it successfully, and was paid with a large sack of flour. No money ever exchanged hands in the village - perhaps they never had any, but to earn more food was very important.

In Siberia, there was no way to buy shoes without a coupon. The Russians who lived there received one coupon per person every year to buy a pair of shoes. However, the 'newcomers' who had been transported to work in the kolkhoz did not qualify for coupons, hence no new shoes. After the shoes they arrived in wore out, they made replacement boots the best way they could: out of a mat or piece of thick felt, rolled and sewed to fit the leg, to which then was attached a makeshift sole with a top. Legs and feet would first be wrapped in rags, and then slid into the makeshift boots. Footwear like this was not comfortable but it kept the cold out.

* * *

Agnieszka's priority was always Roma, now a toddler and running fast, moving fast like her great grandmother. Besides taking total care of little Roma, Agnieszka baked loaves of bread two or three times a week, and often took one or two loaves to a family with children who had even less to eat. She made soups of all kinds. These were her specialty, along with dumplings filled with berries, mushrooms, or even weeds. Sometimes when times were extra hard, she made 'water soup', which consisted of boiling water with a large slice or two of bread crumbled into it.

Her motto was: 'no time to waste.' This small, constantly busy, four-foot-eleven, thin and wiry little woman always wore an apron so as to protect the dress she still had from Poland. She also always wore an impeccably clean scarf tied at her chin to keep her hair out of things and to keep her head warm.

Agnieszka was very resourceful, not only in gathering mushrooms and berries in the forests surrounding the kolkhoz, but also in what could be gathered from the fields. After the harvest, when the gathering and threshing of wheat or oats was done, and all had gone home for the night, Agnieszka would tie her big apron on and go into the fields scooping into the apron grains that have fallen on the ground during the harvesting. What a bonus that was for the soups to come! She was tireless in gathering this treat for her family.

Agnieszka managed to go undetected quite a few times, and then one bright moonlit night, a 'Brigadier' on horseback spotted her, and rode over. Seeing an old grandmother picking up the grains and already a few handfulls in her apron, he told her to "Drop the grains." When she tried to tell him that those would perish with the coming snow, and won't do anyone any good, the response was: "No one steals from Mother Russia...do you know that I could send you to the mines to work for five years for this trespassing and stealing?" Agnieszka had to drop the corner of her apron spilling the grains onto the barren soil. However she did have the last word: she told the man "And who will work on this collective farm when you starve all the imported workers?"

Chapter 4

AMNESTY

In August 1941 the Polish-Russian Military Agreement was signed. In it the main stipulations were (and here I quote from "The Army in Exile"):

A Polish army will be organized as soon as possible on the territory of the U.S.S.R. and this army will become part of the Armed Forces of the Sovereign Polish Republic. . . . It will be destined to take part in the common struggle of the armies of the U.S.S.R. and other Allied Powers against the German Reich. At the end of the war the army will return to Poland. . . .

Polish units will be used at the front when they have reached full preparedness for battle. . . . Soldiers of the Polish army on the territory of the U.S.S.R. will be subject to Polish military laws and regulations. . . . Armament, equipment, uniform, kit, motor vehicles, etc. will be supplied as far as possible, (a) by the government of the U.S.S.R. from their own stocks, (b) by the government of the Polish Republic from supplies obtained under the Lease-Lend Bill.

This agreement was due to the negotiations with the Soviet dignitaries of the first Polish diplomat to arrive in Moscow from London, Dr. Jozef Retinger, on behalf of the Polish Government in Exile, which was based in London.

After the signing of this amnesty agreement, more and more Polish officers and soldiers were released from prisons throughout the Soviet Union and began to report to Moscow.

With great difficulty General Anders, who was to be the acting commander in chief of these released officers and other ranked prisoners of war, obtained permission to organize two Polish divisions and a reserve regiment. The headquarters of the army would be at Buzuluk. The Sixth Division would be stationed at Tatistchev, and the Sixth Division and the Reserve Regiment at Totskoie. But where were the arms, equipment, uniforms, and kits promised them? The Soviet Union provided the minimum. It was impossible to prepare the army for the front against the German Reich.

The Enrollment Commission was sent to the prisoner-of-war camps. But where were the Polish officers? Thousands were missing.

Only at the end of the war was it discovered that Polish officers taken as prisoners—over twelve thousand in number—were murdered by Russians and buried in a mass grave at Katin.

However at this time, with thousands of released prisoners of war who volunteered to join the Polish army, it was necessary to form more divisions, and the Polish army grew daily in numbers. The Soviet authorities were surprised by the huge number of Poles reporting for military service.

Rom was released among other prisoners. He made a decision to cross the border first and see what was happening to his family and home, and then return to the Soviet Union and report to the Polish army base. He was ready to fight the enemies of Poland.

Crossing the border for the second time now, Rom was much more careful, avoiding the border patrols and hiding in the thick forests during the days. With caution, stealth, and patience he made it over the border— this time without any problems.

Chapter 5

ROM LEARNS THAT HIS FAMILY WAS TAKEN TO SIBERIA
ALMOST TWO YEARS AGO

After crossing the border and coming close to the estate grounds, Rom waited until nightfall, hiding in the thickest shrubbery he could find. Hunger had been his companion for the past two days. Now he must rest until the darkness of night, when he could cautiously proceed to the gardener's cottage, a couple of hundred feet behind the manor house, to check on the situation at his father's home and neighborhood.

He had not seen his bride for almost two years. They were married just a year before the outbreak of the war. When Rom was leaving for the front, he urged Janina to close down the town house in Wilno (a beautiful medieval city), where Rom had attended Batory University and where they lived before the outbreak of the war. Then, when war began, he wanted his family to move to the estate of his father in Staro Swieciany. He knew that living in the country during the war would be far safer than staying in the city. He hoped that they would never be hungry there.

Close to his home now, yet in hiding, not knowing if all was well with his family, Rom spent the rest of the daylight hours resting and reminiscing about his youth.

* * *

He was the only son of a wealthy landowner who raised Arabian horses. Rom wanted to go to the Military Academy, but his father insisted on a law career, and once that was accomplished, there would be no objection at all if he still wanted to be an officer. So a couple of years before the war he finally completed the Officers' Army Academy and was in the Reserves.

He spent a lot of his time in Wilno. There he met, pursued, and married Janina, a lovely brunette with green eyes and a regal countenance. He was very much in love, but she was only almost nineteen. Although at first her parents objected that Janina was far too young to marry, after getting to know Rom they relented. Of course his wealth was not a deterrent either. What parents do not wish a life of ease and plenty for their child?

So, the wedding took place. It was a grand military affair, with officers forming a corridor of raised swords through which the bridal couple passed with military pomp and ceremony.

The reception was held in the ballroom of one of the prestigious hotels in Wilno, to accommodate all the family and friends as well as the army personnel invited. All were only too pleased to be invited to such a feast, which Rom's father insisted be his contribution for that memorable day of his son's wedding.

Days before the event sleighs packed with hams, ducks, chickens, geese, and whole little piglets to be spit-roasted as well as liquors were arriving in Wilno from the estate. Finally the day that had long been prepared for and anticipated arrived!

It was also New Year's Day 1939. Many toasts were raised to the young couple and to Poland as well, that both may prosper!

Alas, as the saying goes, something about mice and men making their plans but FATE controlling them.

* * *

Rom's memories were so vivid; for a moment he had been transported to that wonderful day, and he dozed off.

Waking with a start, he realized that dusk was finally falling. "Enough reminiscing; it is time to move on," he told himself. He got up and was reminded again how exhausted and hungry he was.

He circled the estate but could not see anything unusual except that the horses were not in the fields and the manor house seemed neglected. "What else can be expected," Rom thought, "during a time of war?"

Yet he decided to be cautious and go to the gardener's cottage first. Patience and caution were lessons he had learned well. Michal, the gardener, was sitting with his back to the window working on something at the table in front of him. The fireplace burned brightly, lighting up the room. Rom looked around, but there was no one else in sight. He knocked gently on the window and saw Michal turn and stare at him without recognition. "It is me, Rom," he whispered. After peering more closely at him, Michal ran out and quickly pulled Rom inside, looking around with fear to assure himself that there were no witnesses.

Soon Rom learned that the manor house was now in the hands of a new invader, the Russian troops. It was now one of their headquarters, and Rom's father, grandmother, wife, and child had been taken to Siberia close to two years ago.

Michal was quickly filling in the missing links. The Russian troops had come one February night to take the family to the train. The lieutenant in charge had wanted to take only the grandfather and the wife with the child, but the grandmother had insisted that she was going too. Rom smiled; even the Russian officer could not disobey his grandmother.

It was she who had brought him up together with his father, Antoni, when at four years old he lost his mother and two baby sisters to the plague, or black death, that raged through Europe at the beginning of the twentieth century. It was Agnieszka, his grandmother, who had taken care of running the household with a firm but fair hand with all the servants. She was a small but

strong and very capable woman. She always moved and did everything fast, as if every second counted. Rom thought, "Thank God
she is with Janina, the baby, and my father."

Here his thoughts turned to his father, a tall, wiry, strong man
who all his life had worked hard and was self-disciplined and
self-made. He had run the estate and worked alongside his grooms
and farmhands whenever the need arose. By nature he was an optimist, with a smile that came readily to his lips, and when he
worked, his songs often echoed through the meadows. Antoni
loved to sing and had a powerful baritone voice, which, had he
been born at a different time and place, would no doubt have been
trained for the enjoyment of thousands.

Rom asked Michal so many questions that hours passed
quickly. He wanted to know every detail about everything on the
estate.

He knew he must find his family—must cross the border back
to the Soviet Union immediately and find them somehow. There
was no time to lose.

Michal agreed that there was no point in staying there beyond
a day's rest, for Rom could be discovered and imprisoned again.
The crossing of the border had to be done at night, stealthily. He
could not risk being discovered and taken again for a spy.

Michal put together provisions for the return trip: bread, some
dry sausage, fruit, and water were assembled. The peasant had
meager means but willingly gave all he had. He would give everything for the son of his master under whom he had lived peacefully for over thirty years without any worries about where his
food would come from when he grew old. In Antoni's service the
peasants had good and happy lives.

Rom knew that if he wanted to find his family, he needed more than the provisions to hold his body together; he also needed money! He needed things to trade, to be able to grease a hand, if he expected to accomplish anything. That was the way things were done in the Soviet Union.

He knew where his father had buried some gold coins and silver at the beginning of the war. Antoni, as was the case with most landed gentry in those times, did not rely on the banks but kept his money in a safe in his home. His father had accumulated much money in his safe. It was a pity, though, that most was in paper currency, which with the declaration of war had overnight lost its value drastically. Thousands became tens of zlotych (Polish currency). However, one thing had retained its value: the gold.

Antoni had a few dozen gold coins, called "napoleons," worth quite a lot, and with great precaution at the beginning of the war he had buried most of the valuable things in the cherry orchard in chests of strong wood bound with coils of steel. He had divided his treasure so that should it be discovered, not all would be lost at once.

Thus the old silver—trays of various sizes, candelabra, silver tea and coffee services, and other valuable objects—were first carefully packed into big chests. Then one by one each night with two most trusted grooms in his service Antoni had them transported and buried at the end of the large cherry orchard, under each of the six cherry trees, facing the west side of the orchard wall. The gold coins, however, filling a fair-sized pouch, along with a few valuable pieces of jewelry were buried in the cemetery behind his wife's headstone, about three feet down. These were to be the "last resort" money.

Rom, of course, knew all about his father's "safes" in case of need. Now, he thought, was the time of the "last resort."

But the question was how to get them. He could not venture out, not if he wanted to remain free to accomplish the task of going back to the Soviet Union and getting his family out of Siberia and joining the Polish army now being formed there. Yet he must have the coins.

Michal, the faithful gardener, could go to the cemetery any time, even during the day, and no one would pay attention to a peasant digging among the graves. This was quite normal of late, with so many people dying.

So it was decided that Michal would go right away to the cemetery and dig out that pouch of coins and whatever else may be there. As Rom trusted Michal totally, he explained to him exactly where the stash was hidden and asked him to go get it.

Four hours later Michal returned, smiling from the doorway. Indeed, no one had paid the slightest attention to his digging, and though it was with difficulty that the hard soil, still covered with the recent frost, relinquished its treasure, he held it now in a black sack in his hand.

Rom had the coins but now had to figure out how to transport them without being robbed or killed for them. An idea came to him: "sugar cubes," he told Michal. Yes, he would transport them in sugar cubes.

Michal was not enthused about the plan. "So," he replied, "should the guards look in the bag of cubes, they will surely discover the coins." Rom explained that what he needed were the largest sugar cubes on the market and a big bag of them. The ones with the coins would be at the bottom and on top pure sugar ones, which he could even offer to the guards and not worry about it.

Sugar was at a premium during the war years.

Michal was immediately sent off to the market to buy sugar cubes here and there with whatever money he had. "Later I will reward Michal well," Rom thought.

When Michal returned with the sugar cubes, Rom explained that they now needed to scrape out a round section of each cube with a knife and put in each one a gold coin, which was slightly larger than a nickel. After this was done, the cubes were sealed by putting loose sugar over them and pouring water on top drop by drop to set and cement the coins inside. When they were set, Rom and Michal filed the sugar cubes into clean sharp squares. And so twenty-two gold napoleons were enclosed in the sugar cubes. Rom gave a few napoleons to Michal, much against his protestations, to have for his "last resort" when he may need them.

The preparations for the journey back over the border were completed. At about 3:00 A.M. Rom, fed, rested, and dressed like a Polish peasant, with a sack of provisions and a special sack of sugar cubes, set out for yet another life-threatening adventure—crossing the border back into the Soviet Union.

By now somewhat familiar with the border, he made it through with no mishap and started toward the Caspian Sea, where he was informed that the Polish prisoners of war released by declaration of the "amnesty" were gathering by the thousands and waiting to be shipped to the Italian front to fight in the war.

Soon Rom reached an extensive string of camp sites by the Caspian Sea, where thousands of soldiers were being prepared to be shipped to Egypt and Iraq to be battle-trained and then join the Americans and the British fighting in Italy for what would be the last three years of the war.

Rom reported to the headquarters as an officer released from the Moscow political prison and was given the rank of captain. Many fewer officers than soldiers had survived at the hands of the Germans and the Russians, and now officers were needed badly to take on the responsibility of getting the soldiers ready for the battle front again.

Rom, as always, took the responsibility gladly. In the meantime, however, how was he to begin the quest of finding his family? Siberia covered an area almost as large as Europe itself, and all he really knew was that his family had been taken to Siberia. He did not know where or if they were still alive, but he never allowed himself to consider that possibility!

* * *

Some "political" background should be inserted here.

It should always be remembered that Germany and the Soviet Union, by their alliance and joint occupation from the west and the east, intended to end the cause of Poland once and for all—to annihilate not only the Polish state but the living source of the national life.

Germany, however, turned on its Russian ally.

The German attack on the Soviet Union made it possible to sign the Polish-Soviet Agreement, one of the principal aims of which was the creation of a Polish army on Soviet territory to fight the advancing German armies alongside the Soviet Union.

The critical situation forced the Soviet Union to leave the organization of this army in the hands of the Poles themselves.

Before long the Russians realized that the Polish army could never be won for communism, so they made it more difficult for volunteers to report for duty and cut the army rations, hoping thus to reduce its numbers or even to liquidate it altogether. However, because of the help the Russians received from their Western allies, England and the United States, they had to keep on good terms with them and so could not exterminate the Polish troops in the same cruel way they did the prisoners in their camps.

And so General Anders, having his Polish army but without the equipment and ammunition promised by the Russians, persuaded Stalin to agree to the transfer of the Polish army units to the Allied forces in the West via Iran (Persia). This way the allies could equip the Polish army and send it to the war front. After all, Britain and the United States were now the allies of the Soviet Union.

Germany, despite the agreement with the Soviet Union to be allies, was now marching on her, and Western allies were important to the U.S.S.R.

The Soviet Union did not like this turn of events of letting the Polish army leave. Her plan was to send the newly formed divisions of the Polish army, practically unequipped for battle and exhausted by imprisonment, to fight advancing Germans in front of Russian troops; it would have a twofold purpose for Russians: annihilate the Polish divisions and protect their army, who would now be fighting behind the Poles.

But General Anders refused to break up the army this way. He went to Moscow to persuade Stalin that the army as a whole would be welcomed by and useful for the allies to equip and have as a whole to join them against the Germans on the Western front, but not if they were just a few divisions.

It was not a popular plan with Stalin, but he was occupied in defending Moscow from the approaching army of Hitler. It was true that he did not have the promised equipment and ammunition for the Poles while the allies did, so he allowed the Polish army to leave the Soviet Union to strengthen the ranks of the Allied armies to fight Hitler from the Western Front.

Civilians were generally not allowed to leave; only a few thousand attached to the army forces were able to leave with General Anders's Polish army.

So eventually, with the help of the allies, General Anders's army was shipped out from the shores of the Caspian Sea to Pahlevi, a port in Iran. From there it went to the Middle East to train for battle on the terrain of Egypt and Iraq and Africa in order to join the allies, battle-ready and prepared for the Italian front and Monte Cassino and other events up until D-day of 1945.

Out of 1.5 million to 1.6 million Poles who were transported to Siberia either to forced labor camps or prisons, only 115,000 left the U.S.S.R. now. Hundreds of thousands were left behind in prisons or in forced labor camps.

Chapter 6

AT THE ARMY RECRUITMENT CAMP

Although very busy with preparations for his division's shipment out of the Soviet Union, Rom's days were filled also with anxiety about his family and despair at the thought that he might never be able to find them.

Days filled with duty and nights filled with thoughts, always of his family. How would he get them out of Siberia? Where should he begin?

At last, an idea occurred to Rom. If he wrote a short note—oh! hundreds of them!—and asked the men in his division, and even men in other divisions, who knew where their families were in Siberia to please include the note in their letters, and if the note went with hundreds and hundreds of letters to different parts of Siberia, surely someone had heard news of his family.

No sooner had the idea occurred to him, Rom was up and writing, even though looking at his watch, he noticed it was 3:00 A.M. He was not one to procrastinate. Two hours later he had dozens and dozens of such notes ready to distribute to the soldiers and send them on their way.

The note simply said: "If anyone knows of the whereabouts of Michniewicz family, Antoni, Janina, baby Roma and grandmother Agnieszka, please notify Captain Rom Michniewicz."

He knew that if his father heard from him, he would know how to contact Rom, and time was crucial.

At the end of the morning assembly, Rom announced to the troops of his division that he was looking for his wife and child, who had been taken to Siberia in February of 1940. He told the men that he would greatly appreciate it if they would include his note when writing to their families in Siberia. Maybe some family would know or have heard of a lady with a toddler by the name of Michniewicz.

The soldiers who had addresses to write to their families in Siberia immediately came forward to take copies of Rom's note. When these notes ran out, Rom told the men he would have more written by the next day. Over four hundred such notes were finally dispatched via letters to families of the soldiers scattered throughout Siberia.

Weeks went by, and Rom prayed that somewhere someone would have some news of his family before the Polish army shipped out from the Soviet Union.

His prayers were answered. One of his notes arrived in the kolkhoz next to where the Michniewicz family was living. The person receiving the note recognized the name and sent his teenage son to deliver Rom's note to Antoni Michniewicz.

Rom was ecstatic when one day a telegram from his father arrived from a town called Bullayevo in the depth of Siberia. It read: "We are in Kolkhoz X forty kilometers south of Bullayevo. Please come and get us." The signature was that of his father, Antoni Michniewicz.

It took Rom a few days to obtain the necessary documents. Other officers and soldiers who found that their families were in the area where Rom was going asked if he could also remove their wives and sons or daughters. All of a sudden there were eleven families who needed his help. The local authorities provided the documents for all to be brought out of Siberia with Captain Michniewicz.

The military granted Rom the leave necessary to accomplish

his task, but with a very short deadline as the troops were being shipped out steadily. He must not miss the transport out with his division to Iran and on to the Middle East and the war front in Italy.

Rom left for the depths of Siberia equipped not only with travel documents but also with ration cards for provisions of bread and dry fish or sausage. These staples for all connected with military personnel were to be picked up at each station along the way on the return trip. Thank God the military had granted ration cards for eleven families' sustenance along the way! How else would they have managed to eat?

In this time of war, food was worth its weight in gold.

Chapter 7

ROM'S REUNION WITH JANINA AND THE FAMILY

At the end of the day, when the sun was setting, a procession of tired kolkhoz workers was returning from the fields to the village. They walked in groups of three and four, tired but happy, looking forward to a peaceful evening of rest and song after a hard day's work.

At the end of the long snake of people winding up the country road walked a young woman alone. That was Janina.

It had been seven days since the exciting news from Rom reached them. Antoni had gone with the milkman's wagon to the nearest town, Bullayevo, and sent a telegram telling Rom where they were and to come immediately to get them.

No answer had come—nothing.

Janina thought at times that she had imagined all this about Rom coming. It must have been a joke, a cruel joke by someone else. And yet, the note was in Rom's handwriting, so why had there been no word since Antoni had sent the telegram?
Maybe the telegram never left the little town of Bullayevo.

Of course, the Russians did not want anyone to get out of the U.S.S.R. Who then would work in the kolkhoz fields?

Oh God! Janina felt a rising panic.

She walked slowly, ten paces behind the rest. These were not her people; they were the enemy. She thought that if she lived here any longer, she would surely go mad! What about her baby? Roma had been playing with these local children daily, speaking their language. What future would she have in a village like this?

While walking along and musing, she heard someone calling

her name over and over again. She stopped. "Maybe I am already losing my mind," she thought. "I hear Rom's voice." Then again she clearly heard the special name he always called her: "Janusz Janusz!"

She turned, and there he was running toward her calling her name over and over. She stood like a statue, frozen in disbelief.

Rom caught up with her. What joy! What a reunion!

* * *

Earlier that day, when Rom arrived in Bullayevo, he had found a postman's one-horse cart outside the post office. He inquired how he could get to Kolkhoz X and was told he could ride along.

Every week the postman made his rounds to the outlying villages, and today was the day to drive to Kolkhoz X! What luck!

Hours later, as they came to the crest of a hill in this one-horse cart, the postman pointed to a column of workers moving down the hill. "There at the end is the lady, your wife," he told Rom. "She always walks alone, so all here call her 'the lady.'"

Rom had jumped off the cart and run to catch up with his wife, knowing for sure he could get there faster than the one-horse cart, which after many hours of travel was barely moving. After Rom called her name many times, Janina finally turned around and saw Rom.

* * *

The next couple of days were spent telling each other what they had lived through, as well as contacting the eleven families

Janina and Rom walking along a boulevard in Wilno,
Poland (now Vilnius – Lithuania). Rom in the uniform of
the Polish Officers Academy. Year 1937

Our Lady of Ostra Brama in Wilno, Poland (now Lithuania). Both Rom and Janina shared a great devotion to our Lady. This shrine to the Mother of God is famous throughout Poland, and pilgrimages are made to ask for prayers to be answered.

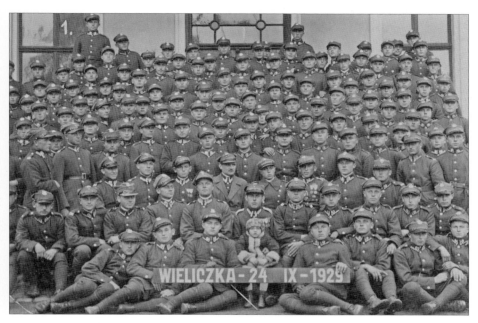

Officers Academy Class. Rom is seated 3rd row from the bottom, 2nd from right.

After an athletic event. Rom sitting in the front, second from the left. The portrait is that of Marshal Jozef Pilsudski, who led the Polish armies to freedom in 1920 at the conclusion of World War I.

Rom with his class. Rom is seated second row from the front, first on the left.

Polish officers enjoying an informal picnic outside the Officers Academy in Wilno.

Rom and Janina's wedding day, New Years 1939, not long before World War II in Poland. It was a military wedding with traditional pomp and ceremony.

The Wedding Party.

The family: Janina, baby Roma and Rom.

Maria and Antoni Michniewicz, Rom's parents. Maria died when Rom was four. Antoni and Grandmother Agnieszka raised Rom.

Example of the cattle cars used to transport exiles from Poland to Siberia. The Michniewicz family travelled like this to Siberia.

The map outlines the route by which we were taken from Vilnius to Siberia. We lived for two years in a kolkhoz, 35 kilometers from Bullayevo which was the nearest town. The downward route shows the way we travelled out of Siberia through Tashkent to Krasnovodsk on the Caspian Sea, and across to Pahlevi in Iran.

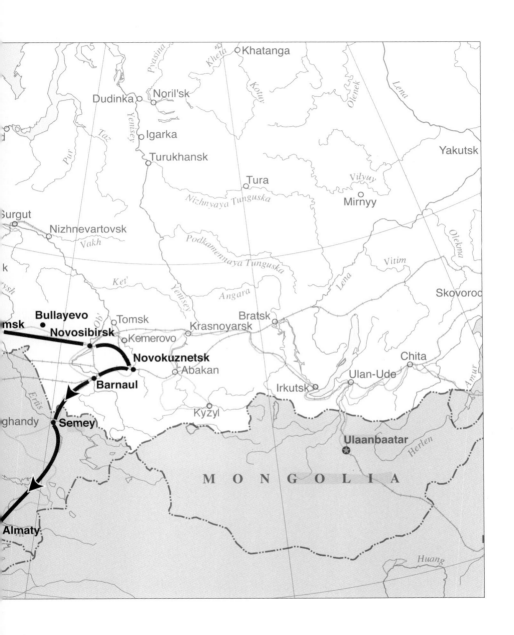

General Wladyslaw Anders – Commander-in-Chief of the Polish forces during World War II.

General K. Sosnkowski and General Wladyslaw Anders in a relaxed moment.

In Italy 1945. Rom top row in the center.

Rom in Italy… serving in the 2nd Polish Army Corps, fighting alongside the British and Americans in WWII.

Janina's identity card photo when leaving Siberia.

Janina's first passport photo.

The Michniewicz family in Lebanon with the addition of baby Peter Zbyszek. Rom was on furlough at the time.

for whose release Rom had brought travel papers: women and children, twenty-four in all, plus Rom's four, adding up to twenty-eight people. All were to meet in Bullayevo railway station in a week. In that short time all the preparations as well as decisions as to what to take and what to leave behind had to be made. One suitcase or box per person at most was allowed, with the rest to be given away to the unfortunates who would stay behind.

The appointed day arrived, and all twenty-eight were gathered at the Bullayevo railway station ready to board the train. Rom had had all the documents duly stamped and notarized by the civilian and military officials from the headquarters of Krasnovodsk by the Caspian Sea, and he presented them here to the station authorities.

Discussion among them ensued, and members of the NKVD were called in. In all fields of civilian and military life, the NKVD (the People's Commissariat of the Interior) was omnipotent in the Soviet Union and greatly feared.

The NKVD browsed through the documents and gave the verdict: "No! No civilian can leave the Motherland. No no, we do not recognize the authorities who issued these documents, and no one can leave. Who would work the kolkhoz farms if we allow the civilians to leave? You, Captain, as a military personnel, can leave. Amnesty was granted to the prisoners of war but not to their families. Oh no, no one else leaves!"

No matter how much Rom explained, used all his skills of persuasion, showed all the credentials again, the decision was final.

Rom arranged for all families to be returned to their homes of the past two years. When he finally arrived at the cottage with his family, he collapsed with a high fever and became delirious. The shock, exhaustion, and anxiety had made his health vulnerable.

For two days there was no improvement, so Antoni took Rom in the milkman's wagon to the hospital in Bullayevo. Rom was diagnosed with typhus and was put in an isolation ward and not allowed any visitors.

For two weeks he was very seriously ill. Antoni and Janina went to the hospital as often as they could to see him but were told, "No visitors; it is an infectious disease."

About two weeks later the disease subsided as suddenly as the fever had come. Although still very weak, Rom checked himself out of the hospital as soon as he could walk unaided.

Back at the cottage, Antoni showed Rom three telegrams that had arrived for him requesting that he report to his division immediately, as they were shipping out of the U.S.S.R. very soon. The last shipment was expected to leave in three weeks. Rom must return at once.

Antoni and Rom discussed the events of the past two weeks, their present situation, and the inability of the civilians to leave Siberia. Antoni told Rom he must take his wife and child out with him or he would never see them again. This was his only chance.

But how was this to be accomplished?

Antoni suggested that as Roma was still relatively small, she could be put in a duffel bag and carried as luggage aboard the trains, and Janina could accompany the captain as a nurse. After all, the captain was just released from the hospital after a serious bout of typhus—it was all in the papers from the hospital. The nurse was to assist him in getting back to base.

So the next day Antoni went with the mailman to Bullayevo and acquired a nurse's uniform with a cape with a big red cross on it. Janina's wedding band was hidden away safely.

Antoni insisted that he and Agnieszka remain where they were. At least they had a roof over their heads and enough to eat and knew the people in the kolkhoz.

Rom strongly objected, but Antoni told him to think about the future his wife and child would have if they were all put out at some God-forsaken station with no shelter and two old people unable to work. It would be easier to travel with just Janina and Roma. Only that way would they have a chance of escaping notice and making it out of Siberia.

Rom tried hard to persuade his father that they could do it together, but Antoni was adamant. He and Agnieszka would stay, and Rom must go with his wife and child. "Now or never," he told his son; he had only one chance to take his wife and child out of Siberia.

One always has choices in life, and each choice one makes shapes one's life. It was the time to make a choice to leave the Soviet Union, even if danger lurked everywhere, for otherwise one stayed there forever.

Once the decision was made, a horse and buggy was hired, and meager provisions were assembled for the journey. Rom decided to go to a more distant town to catch a train, and the three would travel all night through the forest to get there. Otherwise they would likely be recognized in Bullayevo after not being allowed to leave from there just weeks before.

At sunset they loaded the buggy and lined it with hay. Janina and Roma were settled in after saying good-bye to their beloved relatives. Antoni and Agnieszka were to stay behind to give the young generation a chance of escape from Siberia.

Rom held his grandmother and father in a last embrace and then got into the buggy. The horse moved on.

It was perhaps the only time Rom cried in his life, but looking at the two dear figures getting smaller and smaller as the distance took them away, he knew he would never see them again.

And he never did.

Rom, Janina, and Roma traveled through the night and half of the next day through the thick forest to the next small town on the other side. It was not an easy journey. One could sometimes meet wolves or marauders in the depth of the dark forest.

Rom had a loaded revolver in one hand and a long pole with a homemade torch of rags dipped in petrol and lighted to ward off the wolves. It was a long and dangerous journey. They once came across a pack of wolves but were able to keep them at bay with torches. As scared as Janina was, she too waved a lighted torch tirelessly on one side of the cart while Rom took care of the back and the other side. At every howl of the wolves, the horse reared up or bolted wildly, and the horse's jerking moves made the journey doubly perilous. Yet, somehow they made it through the forest.

The three arrived at their destination by the afternoon of the next day. Rom's plan was first to go to the station to get two tickets to anywhere as long as it was going in the direction of the Caspian Sea and as far away as possible before Janina's absence was noted. Antoni had planned to have Janina and Roma supposedly very ill with flu to gain them a few days' start before the authorities discovered that they were actually missing.

So now Rom left his wife and child to wait at the edge of the forest while he went to find the railway station and to check on any train going in their desired general direction away from Siberia.

Chapter 8

JOURNEY OUT OF SIBERIA

After a couple of hours Rom returned with some food and good news that there was a train out of the station the very next day, in the late afternoon. They would stay until then in the forest so as not to arouse any curiosity or suspicion among the people there. The next day Roma would be put inside the duffel bag and carried to the train over Rom's shoulder. Janina, in her nurse's uniform, would accompany them.

Rom would show his documents and papers proving his very recent release from the hospital as well as the telegrams from the army requesting him to "return immediately." One problem that might occur would be the fact that Janina, dressed as a nurse, had no real documents to be accompanying the captain.

Janina took off her wedding ring and put her faith in God.

The rest of that day they took turns sleeping a little, and Roma was quite happy playing around the trees, digging with a broken spoon and "making a garden" just like her great-grandmother used to tend. The child asked often where Nanny and Grandpa were. Obviously she missed them, but how does one explain to a toddler that they were left behind? She still had the little basket, empty now, that her grandfather had given her full of peas and carrots from the garden on the day they left. The child was not aware that she would not see these loving people ever again, and not knowing was her blessing.

Since Great-grandmother Agnieszka had taken care of Roma for the past two years, Janina was not as well attuned to the child's needs. She was young herself and easily frightened by every sound.

When it was time to go to the station, they packed their meager belongings. Janina carried a bag tied with a string that held the fur coat she had worn when she arrived in Siberia. Grandfather had called it "the item of last resort," to be sold in dire emergency.

They approached the checkpoint and, surprisingly, were ushered through.

Once the three were on the train, the duffel bag was laid on the top bunk, and Janina lay in front of it on her side so little Roma could be behind. There was barely enough room for them on the narrow, single wooden bunk. Rom took the bottom bunk. The train started, and they were on their way.

A few hours later a conductor with the NKVD came through for another check of people's tickets and documents. Janina froze with fear but covered herself and the child with the Red Cross cape and pretended to be asleep. She prayed they would not be discovered.

The NKVD man looked carefully at Janina and said to Rom, "She is your wife, and you are trying to smuggle her out, right?" Rom replied, "She is just a nurse accompanying me to base." "Uh huh," granted the conductor, unconvinced.

Rom knew that his family was in danger. They could be taken off the train and questioned, and then little Roma would be discovered. He would be ordered to proceed to join the army, but he knew that if that happened, Janina and Roma would be put out at the next station. They could not survive alone.

He knew what he must do. The train had scheduled stops periodically for water, about every five to seven hours, at deserted places where there was nothing except huge barrels of water. They must get off at the next water stop to save themselves. The

NKVD officials would not just rest on their suspicions and sooner or later would arrest the family.

Rom and Janina watched in anticipation for the next water stop, but it was hours before they saw it. Finally the train began to slow down. The family went and stood by the door, and as the train lost speed, Rom jumped off. Running alongside the train, he took Roma in the duffel bag from Janina, along with the rest of their meager luggage, and then helped Janina off just as the train screeched to a halt. Roma was released from the duffel bag, and Rom, carrying the child and a bag of provisions, ran toward a wooded area, encouraging Janina to hurry, hurry. They must hide.

They lay low to the ground for what seemed to them an intolerable amount of time while they waited to see if anyone noticed that they were missing. But no one had expected them to get off in the middle of nowhere.

All was quiet, and the train moved on. But where were they?

Rom decided it would be best to backtrack to the last small station they had passed some time ago. There he would find out where they were exactly. But backtracking with Janina and Roma would be impossible and would require much more time. Rom decided he would go alone.

But he could not leave Janina and Roma on the ground under the trees. Wolves could come at night. For safety he had to get them up into a tree. He looked around and saw a massive tree with low branches for access and assisted first Janina and then Roma to climb up. Then he went up and settled them as comfortably as he could. To make sure Roma would not fall, he tied her in between Janina and the branches with the rope that had previously tied their belongings.

Rom told Janina not to expect him back for a day at least and not to come down from the tree for any reason, not even to retrieve any possessions that might fall down. He assured her that wolves would not climb the tree.

Leaving these instructions, as well as the food and their possessions, Rom set out to find that station, which he calculated would be about twenty kilometers or so from where they were.

Following the railway tracks so as not to lose his way, jogging and walking alternately, he finally arrived at the little railway station. There he was told that there were no trains going in the direction he wanted, only in the opposite direction. He caught the first train going in the opposite direction and in three hours arrived at a much larger station. There he hoped to have a better chance of traveling where he needed to go.

He had among his documents the military ration card that allowed him to collect at each large station the provisions of fish and bread for the people who were supposed to be traveling with him. He went immediately in search of the canteen that dealt with rations for the military. Rom was always very confident and at ease with people in general, and so he did not have any trouble collecting a bag of dried smoked fish and a dozen loaves of bread. Now he had bartering power.

Rom located the conductor of the train that would be traveling in the direction his family needed to go. By giving him most of his rations as a bribe, Rom secured arrangements for his family to board the train the next day. When it stopped for a few minutes at the watering place, he, Janina, and Roma would be waiting to quickly board the train.

Rom took the same train that they as a family would board tomorrow. As it slowed near the water station, he jumped off without anyone noticing and hurried to his family.

* * *

Janina had begun to despair some hours earlier that Rom must have been caught and would never return. She had decided that if this were the case, they would die up in the tree. She vowed never to venture out of that tree if Rom did not return.

At night she heard wolf packs around the tree and saw their glowing eyes in the darkness. Better to die of starvation and cold up in the tree than come down and be eaten alive by the beasts.

* * *

What joy there was when Rom appeared, and brought food! They were ravenous! Even little Roma ate smoked fish and bread with great appetite.

The next day they prepared to go to the water station at the hour when the long-distance fast train would be passing by. This time they did not put Roma in a duffel bag. They would travel to the next, bigger station some two days away just as they really were, a family.

The train stopped as scheduled, and the conductor even helped them aboard. They were off continuing their journey out of Siberia. While on board they slept and ate and slept again.

After they reached the station and left the train, the family again hid in the neighboring forest. In town there were patrols examining the documents of passersby. Rom and his family could not risk being discovered.

This time when Rom went to collect the rations, he came away with some sausages and twelve loaves of bread. Again he had bargaining power: food.

He found out that all major trains were heavily guarded and that NKVD officials were constantly checking papers and passports and taking poor souls into custody. There had to be an alternate route, somehow.

Rom learned that once a week there was a water train going by this way, not actually stopping but passing by. So as not to spill the water out of great, ten-thousand-gallon water barrels, which swayed on their platforms as the tracks wound around the bends of the mountainous terrain, the train traveled very slowly. It would slow down even more around a sharp bend, and that was the best place to jump on and hitch a ride.

Rom went some ten kilometers outside the little town and waited to watch a water train pass by, observing its path as it circled around the township and continued slowly up the winding trail. Over a period of several days he watched the trains and figured out the best place to board.

Yes, right down the mountain and turning before town, the train really slowed down going around a sharp bend. That was the place to wait for the next water train and get on. He would hoist Janina up onto the three-foot platform around the barrels and then pass Roma to her. Then, when the train was already gathering speed, he would jump aboard.

He would need to acquire provisions and a thick rope of fair length this time in order to tie all of them to a huge water barrel to prevent them from falling off in case they fell asleep during the night. He would also search for something at the street market to keep them warm during the cold nights. The food rations and some napoleons he had in sugar cubes would make the purchases possible.

He was told that the water train took three days to reach the next town. Siberia is a vast land mass.

Rom bartered for all the things required for the trip the best he could. Again the food rations he was able to collect at the army depot proved to be the best for goods exchange. Water would be plentiful since the barrels spilled quite a bit each time the train rounded a bend. All they needed was a container to catch it in, and also some improvised shelter to keep them from being drenched constantly by the spilling cold water.

The day arrived when they were at the chosen boarding place to jump onto the water train. As soon as the train began to slow down, Janina and Rom ran alongside, and Rom lifted his wife up onto the platform. Next he ran to get the child, who already was running after her parents quite unable to understand why they were running away from her.

Rom lifted the child up to Janina, who held her tightly. After gathering the packages containing the food, rope, and animal skins he had purchased to keep them warm, plus Janina's packed fur, and passing them all to Janina, he jumped onto the train as it was picking up speed.

First of all, it was very important to tie all of them to a barrel with the thick rope he had purchased. While Janina held one end of the rope, Rom crawled around the big barrel with the other, coming full-circle to tie them all as securely as possible. The water began to spill around each curve of the tracks, drenching them all. They had little Roma between them, and although trying hard to stay dry, they got thoroughly soaked quite often.

Even so, they felt safe and were together. There was food and water, and they were on their way out of Siberia. They were happy. God made all things possible. Life was looking better and better.

Faith in God was their source of strength.

On the third day Rom knew it was time to think of disembarking this floating transport. As the train rounded the mountain, they saw an outline of a town in the distance and readied themselves to jump off before reaching the town.

Rom jumped off first and started running alongside the train. He then grabbed Roma and sat her on the ground. Janina tossed the baggage off and leaped into Rom's arms. They had arrived somewhere going in the right direction but yet still far from the end of their journey.

After settling the family in a field of tall grasses and shrubs, Rom went to the town, which turned out to be farther away than he anticipated. His return was not until late by moonlight, but he had a plan.

The situation was that, as before, he needed to catch the train going in the opposite direction the next day and bribe the conductor to be able to get his family on the train in town down below so that they could proceed forward-bound.

The next morning the three of them set out for the town, a journey that took them half the day, with frequent rest periods for the ladies. At dusk Rom settled his family in the railway station with hundreds of people sleeping on the platforms and hoping to get on a train. Janina and Roma were settled by the wall of the stationmaster's office and at least felt safer there than in the forest.

Rom caught a train in the opposite direction to a larger town. After getting the rations of food, he was able to bribe the conductor to allow him and the family to board the train when it arrived the next day at the station where they were waiting. Then he doubled back, and the family waited together to continue their journey.

Time passed uneventfully. As evening approached, they made their way close to the end of the tracks and waited. The train arrived, and crowds started pushing and shoving toward the doors, but the conductors barred the way. Rom, with Roma in his arms and Janina close behind, ran toward the last car, where the conductor whom Rom bribed was supposed to allow them to board. He lifted Roma up, at the same time saying, "I am Captain M, and here is my family as we arranged."

In response a leather boot hit Roma in the chest and a screaming conductress yelled, "No one gets in! No one!"

Rom looked up and realized that this was not the same person he had given all those provisions to in order to assure that his family could board this train.

The child was crying as Rom tried to tell the conductress that he had a bag of provisions he could give her at the next stop if only she would let them board. But unmoved, she was already calling for the police.

Rom realized that it was a lost cause this time. Meanwhile Janina, as instructed, had already tossed their luggage through the open window of the train compartment they were trying to enter.

The whistle blew, and the train began to move forward. At that moment Janina cried, "Our bags, my fur! I put them through the window as you told me to!" As he ran after the departing train, Rom shouted, "I will return tomorrow. Wait at the same place by the stationmaster's!" She saw him hop with great effort onto the back stair of the train and climb to the platform before the train disappeared from sight.

A long night and day passed before they saw Rom coming toward them holding the two bundles that were their luggage. He was exhausted and had to rest most of that day and again the following day. After getting more rations he caught a train back to the previous town so that this time he could bribe two conductors in case they changed shifts. After what seemed an eternity to Janina, he returned.

Again they waited to board the train. This time, with the assistance of the conductress Rom had first bribed, they were allowed to board.

They were again moving forward. Rom was beginning to worry that it was taking much longer than he had counted on. What if they arrived too late? What if the troops had shipped out already?

What would happen to them if the last shipment of troops had departed? No more food rations and no legal documents for Janina and the baby.

But Rom had faith that God would take care of things and help them get out of Siberia. He was always a great optimist. If things did not go as planned, well, there were always alternatives.

If they reached the Caspian Sea at Krasnovodsk, they would be closer to Poland and could then cross the border into that country. But there Rom would most probably be imprisoned, as this part of Poland was now Russian territory. They had no home now in Poland. In spite of his fears that the troops would ship out without him, he hoped that the family would make it to the Caspian Sea and out of the U.S.S.R. and that he could fight again for the freedom of Poland, his beloved country.

Meanwhile, his family would be safe living somewhere in the free world until the time they could all return home, to a free Poland.

They were again traveling through the Urals, beautiful mountain ranges, passing through countless villages, kolkhozes, towns ravaged by war. Everywhere the train slowed down, hundreds of people, more like beggars than citizens of any country, tried to push their way onto the train. But the doors were firmly locked, and gun barrels were freely used to shake off those hanging on to the steps.

Poor, sad humanity trying to escape their condition. Their homes had been burned by the retreating Germans. Starvation was imminent for those who stayed behind, old and young alike.

After three days the conductor came to tell Rom that the train would stop at the next station and, after picking up the supplies, would then turn around and go back.

Again, time to get off and try to go forward to escape from Siberia.

Rom, Janina, and Roma got off and quickly mingled with the throngs of bedraggled people. Mixing with the crowd was the best way to remain undetected. Again, Rom found a corner near the station where Janina and Roma could sit with the baggage while he went to get the food rations that would make possible their passage out of Siberia.

Food could buy anything.

Rom found out that in two days there would be a train going to Tashkent. From there it would be about a two-day journey to Krasnovodsk, the largest city close to the Caspian Sea—and close to the camps of the Polish army awaiting the Allied ships that would transport them out of the Soviet Union.

Rom did not anticipate any further problems from Tashkent on to Krasnovodsk. He had the documents that would be recognized there, although he still worried secretly that he would not be in time to make the last transport out of the U.S.S.R.

Rom went about obtaining two tickets for the journey to Tashkent, a distance of three days. The waiting at the station seemed unending. This time little Roma must again board the train in the duffel bag slung over his shoulder like a piece of luggage.

The larger station would have more police checking order papers and documents. Janina must put on her Red Cross cape and cap and appear to be a nurse accompanying the captain to his army base by the Caspian Sea. After all, Rom had a few telegrams requesting him to return immediately to base. He did not look well—no wonder, with what he had gone through in the last few weeks—so it should be no surprise that the nurse had to accompany him.

The day of departure arrived, and just before entering the station, little Roma was put into the duffel bag and told to be very

very quiet. The child seemed to understand and instinctively put her trust in her Daddy. They were ready.

At the gate to the station Rom had to show his papers. No problem; they were allowed to pass. On the platform while waiting for the train, again there were random checks of papers, and again they passed the inspection.

At last the train arrived, and they were allowed to board under the watchful eyes of the NKVD. They settled in the compartment, putting the duffel bag on the top bunk. Janina climbed up immediately to lie on her side in front of it. Roma could then get her head out and breathe freely. Rom settled on the bottom bunk. Soon more military personnel took the spare seats.

No one spoke to anyone. One never knew who among them might be a spy and inform the authorities.

The train began to move.

A couple of hours passed peacefully. Rom had just begun to relax when the door opened and three NKVD officers walked in. "Papers please," rang the usual command. The oldest of the three was a colonel, and the others were officers of lower rank. When Rom produced his papers, the colonel looked at the nurse on the top bunk and said: "It is quite obvious to me that the young woman here is your wife, Captain, and not a nurse. We don't send nurses to accompany anyone dismissed from the hospital. Yes, she is your wife. You will have to get off at the next station, and there the matter will be investigated." With this he returned Rom's papers to him, and the three NKVD officers left the compartment.

Rom was in shock. He knew the investigation would mean discovery of the child. He would be sent to his destination, but the authorities would keep Janina and the child in the Soviet Union. Under the present law only prisoners of war, not civilians, received amnesty. God, what would happen to Janina with a toddler left in a large city where she knew no one? They would perish from hunger and disease on the streets. He had three days to come up with a plan. But what?

Rom walked the corridors all night and the next day, hardly sitting down for a rest and eating very little. He had no idea this time how to get his family out of this predicament.

They say people go gray under great stress, and that was proven true. Half of Rom's hair turned gray in just thirty hours. He was only thirty-three years old.

Janina cried and looked out of the window at the passing scenery with unseeing eyes. Her thoughts were in turmoil. She should have stayed in the village with Antoni and Agnieszka. There they had enough food, however poor they were, and a warm place to sleep. What would happen to them now?

They would be on the streets or, worse, in prison for disobeying the law. She was incapable of rational thought or speech. She had no consoling words for her husband. In fact, she blamed him. He should have realized they had no way of getting out of Siberia without proper documents! He should have known better. She always depended on him.

Thus began the third day of the journey, each hour bringing them closer to their unknown fate.

Rom had his watch on his wrist hidden from public view by his uniform. He had smuggled it out in the heel of his boot when he took the gold coins from his father's estate. It seemed an eternity away now, but he calculated that it was approximately only two months ago.

Suddenly he made a decision. He must talk with the colonel and tell him he was married a short time before the war broke out. Until just a month ago he had not seen his wife or child for two and a half years. He would ask the colonel if he had a wife and children and tell him about little Roma in the duffel bag. After all, the authorities would know about her twelve hours from now. He would ask him as a man, as a fellow officer, would he not have done the same in his place? Would he not have tried to get his family out of Siberia?

Rom made his way to the first-class compartments, but the passage was barred by two guards with revolvers. No one could pass beyond this point. Rom explained that he needed to speak with the colonel, that it was a matter of great urgency. At first the guards would not listen and told Rom that the colonel was a very busy man. But Rom did not give up. Never before had his knowledge of the Russian language been so useful.

Rom used many arguments, insisting that he had some knowledge that the colonel needed to be informed of immediately. After much argument, one of the guards went to ask the lieutenant if the colonel should be disturbed or not. The lieutenant interrogated Rom too, but Rom insisted that he would discuss the matter only with the colonel.

At last he was led toward the colonel's compartment and waited anxiously outside while the lieutenant relayed the matter to his commanding officer. Rom was admitted and faced the colonel.

"Well, what do you have to tell me?" the colonel asked.

Rom summarized the past three years, his imprisonment twice, his family taken to Siberia

"I am a busy man," replied the colonel. "I'll give you ten minutes to tell me something of importance. What I am hearing so far is what every soldier experiences at the time of war."

Rom pulled his sleeve up to glance at the watch. He must make every second count. As he looked up at the colonel, he noted the officer's quick glance at his watch. Yes, the watch was gold and impressive; even the bracelet was gold, of excellent mark. Rom had received it from his father on the day of his graduation from the Officers' Academy. The inscription on the back read: "I am proud of you. Serve your country well. Dad."

Having caught the eye of the colonel, his mind quickly grasped the concept. He would try a bribe—he had nothing to lose now.

Rom took the watch off quickly and, handing it to the colonel, asked, "Would you like this?"

"Why didn't you say so at the beginning?" replied the colonel as he reached for the watch. He inspected it with an eye of someone who knew the worth of an object.

"You and your family will not be put out at the next station. You may proceed to Tashkent, and from there you should have no problems. That will be all, Captain."

Rom was dismissed.

Rom ran to the compartment where Janina sat quietly crying. He shouted, "It is fine, it is all fine. We are free!"

"His mind has been affected by all that's happened," she thought. He sat beside her, hugged her, and explained quickly how the gold watch had bought their passport to freedom. Roma was taken out of the duffel bag and looked from one parent to the other while they hugged her and each other and cried and laughed alternately.

When they arrived in Tashkent, the three could proceed openly as a family. They boarded the first train to Krasnovodsk and headed west.

How different this last lap of the journey was. They sat at a table in comfortable chairs and ate their first proper meal in weeks. This dining car was reserved for the officers and their families.

This was heaven! People were talking and laughing. They introduced themselves around and exchanged tales of their adventures. All the others were from far away, but not from the ends of the Siberian steppes where Rom had rescued his family.

Rom found out that his division was shipping out in two days and that the families would stay and occupy the camp while waiting to be shipped to countries that were willing to take immigrants or displaced persons for the duration of the war. After the war, all hoped to return to their own, free country—Poland.

Upon arrival at the military camp, there was little time for long good-byes. Rom had his instructions and duties to perform. A day later an American warship transported the last divisions of the battalion from Russian soil to join the war front via Iran, Iraq, Egypt, Africa, and on to Italy.

Attached to the Second British Corps, Rom fought in many

battles alongside the British and American forces, culminating in the battle for Monte Cassino and Angona. He survived the war and joined his family in England.

Three months after arrival on the shores of the Caspian Sea, after living in army tents with hundreds of family members of the Polish forces, Janina and Roma were taken to the city of Isfahan in Iran. From there they were sent to other countries willing to host the refugees and finally, after the end of the war, to England, where Rom awaited them.

Hundreds of other Polish families went to South Africa, England, Argentina, Spain, or other countries that offered to take displaced persons coming from the Soviet Union who could not return to their homeland.

Now Poland was under the Communist regime, and all those who served with the British or American forces would be imprisoned should they return.

* * *

Little Roma is me. I have recently retired from UCLA, where I worked for nearly thirty years as an academic adviser to the Departments of Art and Graphic Design.

In one lifetime, I have lived in many countries and had four nationalities: Polish, English, New Zealander, and now American.

But that is another story.

Roma King

Postscript

Why We Could Not Return to Poland

After the war, we did not have a free Poland after all. Despite fighting alongside the Allied forces and promises from them, the Polish army did not achieve its aim, freedom for Poland, which was now Communist.

I feel it is very important to give here a synopsis of the reason why the Polish troops could not return to their native land as was their hope. The reason was the Yalta settlement-agreement:

The three heads of government from Great Britain, the United States, and the Soviet Union settled among themselves that the eastern frontier of Poland should follow the Curzon Line (aka the Iron Curtain) and would be given to the Soviet Union. Our allies made that decision behind our backs. Churchill, Roosevelt, and Stalin recognized that Poland must receive substantial accessions of territory in the north and west, previously Germany, but that the final delineation of the western frontier of Poland should await the Peace Conference. And yet they gave the eastern half of Poland to the Soviet Union without awaiting the Peace Conference. As part of the Yalta agreement, it was also stipulated by Churchill that the new Provisional Polish Government of National Unity would be set up, with the Soviet Union having an active part in it.

The next day the Polish government in London made a public protest at this partition of Poland by her two allies. Polish troops in Italy also objected to the Yalta decision. The impact the agreement had on all Poles, both at home and abroad, was shattering. It meant that the eastern half of Poland, including Lwow and Vilno, territory that had been closely connected with Poland for over six hundred years and which had never had any Russian population, was to be seized by the Soviet Union. Polish constitutional law was to be violated, and the lawful government, which had cooperated with the allies throughout the war, was to be thrust aside to make way for one organized by Moscow.

Field Marshal Alexander gave an explanation that one potent factor in this decision was that the Soviet Union was in actual occupation of practically the whole of Poland. He further stated that the British wanted to support a free and independent Poland. It may have been so, but nevertheless, the Yalta agreement had been signed by Churchill in the name of Great Britain, and Poland was neither free nor independent.

A couple of weeks later Commander in Chief General Anders met with Churchill. Following is the transcript of their meeting:

Churchill: "You are not satisfied with the Yalta conference."

General Anders: "It is not enough to say that I am dissatisfied. I consider that a great calamity has occurred. The Polish nation did not deserve to see matters settled the way they have been, and we who have fought on the Allied side had no reason to expect it. Poland was the first to shed her blood in this war and sustained terrible losses. She was an ally of Great Britain from the very beginning and throughout the most crucial times. Abroad we made the greatest effort possible in the air, on land and sea, while at home we had a most important resistance movement against the Germans. Our soldiers fought for Poland, fought for the freedom of their country. What can we, their commanders, tell them now? The Soviet Union, [which] until 1941 was in close alliance with Germany, now takes half our territory, and in the rest of it she wants to establish her power. We know by experience what her intentions are."

Churchill: "It is your own fault. For a long time I advised you to settle frontier matters with the Soviet Union and to surrender the territories east of the Curzon Line. Had you listened to me the whole matter would now have been different. We have never guaranteed your eastern frontiers. You can take away your divisions. We shall do without them."

General Anders: "That is not what you said during the last few years. We still want to fight for Poland, free and independent. The Soviet Union has no right to our territory, and she never questioned our possession of it. She broke all treaties and grabbed these territories on the strength of an agreement and an alliance with Hitler. There are no Russians in these territories. Apart from Poles there are only Ukrainians and White Ruthenians. You understand that the elections of so called government in 1939 under the pressure of Russian bayonets were a sheer mockery."

The decisions of Yalta were a crime against the Polish nation.

Also due to the Yalta agreement, it came to pass that on June 28, 1943, the new Provisional Polish Government of National Unity was set up, with three-quarters of its members being imposed by the Soviet Union, many of them not even Polish citizens, while a silent world condoned this crime against Poland.

On July 6, 1943, the British House of Commons welcomed the establishment of the Polish Provisional Government of National Unity and informed that government of their readiness to establish diplomatic relations. Thus the Polish president, Mr. Raczkiewicz, who in 1940 had been greeted at Paddington Station by King George VI; the Polish government in London; and the Polish forces, who had fought so long on the side of Great Britain and the United States, were discarded. In 1940 Mr. Churchill had assured General Sikorski that Poland and the allies were bound together in this war for life or death. But the Soviet Union was much stronger than these promises.

The Potsdam conference, which began on July 17, 1945, marked yet another step on the part of Britain and the United States toward the "appeasement" of the Soviet Union. It was stated that the three powers were anxious to assist the Polish Provisional Government in facilitating the return to Poland as soon as practicable of all Poles abroad who wish to go, including members of the Polish Armed Forces and the Merchant Navy.

The three heads of governments also agreed, "pending the final determination of Poland's western frontier," to the shifting of that frontier to the west—to the line that it occupies today—and the immediate transfer to the Soviet Union of the northeastern portion of East Prussia with Konigsberg.

Soon after the Potsdam conference, the British government had told the Polish ambassador, Count Raczynski, that it had ceased to consider the Polish president as the supreme head of the Polish armed forces and that it would also cease to recognize the commander in chief of the Polish army.

The response to the British government was as follows:

"Polish Armed Forces, linked to His Majesty's Armed Forces by agreements and comradeship in arms for over five years of war, are in accordance with the provisions of the Polish Constitution subordinated to the supreme authority of the President of Poland. They have never ceased to consider the legal President of Poland as their constitutional head, to whom they are pledged by oath and by soldier's faith. In spite of the fact that this state of things is no longer recognized by the British side, the Polish Armed Forces are confident that the President of Poland will be treated with respect and hospitality."

Such was the end of the Allied friendship.

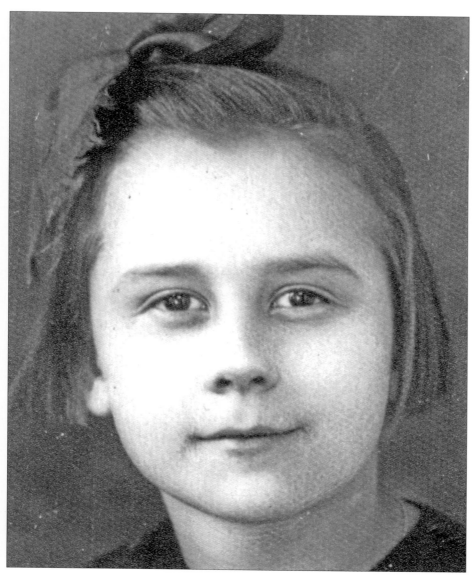

Young Roma, Rom's daughter, in Iran

Young Kathy, Rom's granddaughter in the USA

Rom in New Zealand, 1977

Rom 1977 in New Zealand.

Rom relaxing on a friend's boat on vacation in California.

Rom and Janina in New Zealand 1978

Roma and Janina 2006 outside Janina's home in Sydney Australia, 2006

Janina, Roma and Peter Zbyszek Michniewicz in Australia, celebrating Janina's 90th
Birthday.

Janina's 91st Birthday, 2007

Roma and Janina on Janina's 91st birthday.

Roma and Janina on Janina's 92nd Birthday.

Janina with her greatly loved granddaughter Kasienka (Kathy).

Three generations – Kathy Barrett, Grace Barrett, David Barrett and Roma King at Roma's home in California, 2006.

Roma with grandchildren Grace and David Barrett in Los Angeles, California.

Top: Rom and Janina's great grandchildren.
Bottom: The young athlete. How proud Rom would have been to have an athlete in
the family, great-grandson, David Barrett, 2008

Grace Barrett, great-granddaughter in Polish national costume.

Roma, Kathy and Grace at the International Festival in San Diego.

Roma King, daughter, in Polish national costume.

Rom and Janina's great grandchildren: Grace and David Barrett, 2009

Roma King and Katherine (King) Barrett visiting Poland for the first time, 1985

Katherine (King) Barrett and Roma King, 2008

The Barrett Family 2009. Kathy, David Sr., David Jr., and Grace.

Stephen and Roma.

Rom and Janina's gravestone. Janina drew, chiseled and painted the forget-me-nots on Rom's marble headstone: a labor of love, which she executed patiently and with great precision.

One more fact needs to be told:

On June 8, 1946, the Victory Parade was held in London. The Polish forces, who had been the first to fight the Germans and who even in the worst days had never deserted their allies, were not invited to take part, as that would not have been politically expedient. An invitation was, however, extended to twenty-five airmen from among those Polish airmen who had such a big share in the Battle of Britain. The airmen declined, for they did not wish to represent the Polish forces at a ceremony from which the navy and the army had been excluded. The attitude of the British authorities caused the Poles, and especially the Polish soldiers, to feel more embarrassment than anger toward an ally to whom they had been bound by the brotherhood of arms.

However, at Ancona, Italy, the Polish Army Corps on June 15 celebrated Soldier's Day. After Mass, the commanders of each unit present read the text of the vow here quoted:

"According to the decision of our Allies with whom we fought side by side all the time for the common cause of freedom, the Independent Polish Forces are to demobilize. . . . Today the world understands that Poland is ruled by servile agents of Moscow. . . .

We are deeply convinced that we were always loyal to our Allies at times most perilous for them. In spite of this, however, there were no Polish soldiers parading on V-Day. The Polish airmen, who were the only ones to be invited, refused to take part in the celebration as the Polish sailors and soldiers from Monte Cassino were absent. . . . As soldiers of the sovereign Polish Republic, who remain faithful to their oath, we vow before God, our colors and the graves of our comrades, that in unity with the aims of the whole nation, both in Poland and abroad, we shall continue our struggle for the liberty of Poland, regardless of the conditions in which we shall have to live and work."

The text of that vow was signed by General Anders on behalf of the soldiers of the Second Polish Army Corps.

On the hilltop above the Polish Military Cemetery at Monte Cassino there stands a beautiful and dignified little inscription:

> *We Polish soldiers*
> *For our freedom and yours*
> *Have given our souls to God*
> *Our bodies to the soil of Italy*
> *And our hearts to Poland.*

Thus a chapter in Polish history came to an end.

And so Rom, an officer and a soldier, after fighting in the Second Polish Army Corps and surviving major battles, became now a soldier without a country, a man to whom the road to his home was barred forever.

Rom died in November 1979, never again after 1939 being able to revisit free Poland.

THE END

ACKNOWLEDGEMENTS:

I would like to acknowledge and thank from my heart Stephen Kania for scanning many photographs for me and proof reading my story with patience and tact, even when I refused to make the changes saying:'that is the way I talk'...and I am the author, and so have the prerogative to do it 'my way'...

I would like to acknowledge and thank most sincerely for the work my dear friend Paul Martinez has put into designing the cover of this book and scanning and organizing all the photographs...and
preparing 'print ready' my little book.

I am deeply indebted to Stephen and Paul and am very grateful for the assistance, without which it would take me forever to finish this project...

I would also like to thank my publisher, Jurek Wierzbicki, for his patience and guidance and assurance 'that the quality of the printing will be of the highest standard'...and it is.

With gratitude and indebtedness to my 3 Gentlemen.

Final proof reading was done by Katherine (King) Barrett my brilliant, wonderful daughter. Thank you darling.

Roma King

Roma King was born in Poland. She lived with her Parents in eight countries before settling in the United States, in the Los Angeles area.

After teaching Junior High School and working in a law firm for several years, Roma became an Academic Advisor for the Departments of Fine Arts and Design/Media Arts at UCLA. She loved her work.

Recently, after almost thirty years working with UCLA students, Roma has retired. She now devotes all her time to her family, friends and travel. She also volunteers for many community projects.

Roma has written 3 children's books: "Safari", "My Guardian Angel" and "Grace Makes Potato Pancakes".